Focus on Famous Women

Indira Gandhi

Rose of India

72 69

CAROL BAUER CHURCH

Greenhaven Press, Inc.
1611 POLK ST. N.E. MINNEAPOLIS, MINNESOTA 55413

PHOTOGRAPHIC CREDITS

Indian Embassy: Cover, 2, 4, 5 (top and bottom), 7, 57, 63.
Nehru Memorial Museum and Library: 9, 11, 13, 15, 19, 21, 27,
34, 39, 41, 43, 51.
**Photo Division, Ministry of Information and Broadcasting,
Government of India:** 17, 23, 29, 32.
United Press International Photos: 47, 49, 54, 59, 61.
Wide World Photos: 53.

© 1976 by Greenhaven Press, Inc.

ISBN 0-912616-43-1

Table of Contents

Indira Gandhi
Rose of India

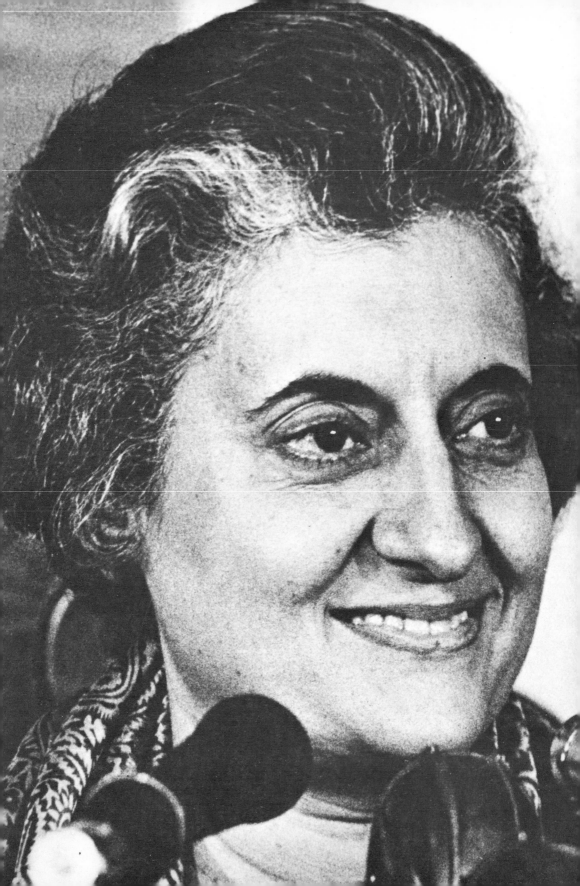

Introduction –

The Mystery of India

The most powerful woman in the world leads India, a land of 600 million people.

What is India? It is a country the size of Europe with fourteen main languages. Millions of its people live in mud huts, trying to grow their food on small plots of ground. If the rains fail, the people starve. Thousands bed down on the streets of cities because they have nowhere else to sleep. India is a poor country.

It is also a rich country with beautiful cities and buildings dating back to 700 A.D. It is rich with religious beliefs and feasts, customs and culture which form a big part of its people's lives.

Nothing we know compares with the mystery which is India. How can we describe it?

Five blind men were asked to touch an elephant and tell what they felt. One man touched its tusks, one its trunk, one its leg, one its tail, and one its side.

Each person described the elephant from his own point of view. Like the elephant, India shows a different face to each person who looks at it.

The most powerful woman in the world leads this country. Her name is Indira Nehru Gandhi. This is her story.

1

The Rosebud Returns

If you work in the sun and in the light, my dear, you will grow up as a child of the light, unafraid, whatever may happen.

Indira stood in the doorway of her father's office. His desk and belongings were just as he had left them. She missed him. The twenty months since his death had been lonely. More than once she had remembered his words and had become peaceful.

Today was the big election. She had been asked to run for the post her father held for nineteen years, that of prime minister, the leader of India.

"Are you willing to carry the heaviest load ever carried by a woman in history?" she had been asked.

What could she say? Like Joan of Arc, her heroine of freedom, she wanted to lead her people.

She had answered, "I am willing."

The Prime Minister of India, Indira Nehru Gandhi, was elected in 1966.

Jawahar (second from right) is pictured
with his parents, Motilal and Swarup, his
little sister, and his uncle (on the left).

She walked slowly back to her home, deep in thought.
There she picked a red rose and pinned it to her white
sari. Her father had been called a ''rose in human form.''
He had always worn a rosebud.

The house of Parliament from which leaders elected by
the Indian people governed the huge country was in
confusion and excitement as she entered. Over five
hundred members were there to cast their votes. Indira
greeted several members with hands folded together
under her chin and a slight bow. Then she took her seat.

Outside the hall thousands of people waited for four
hours. As the voters began to leave, shouts rose up.

''Is it a boy or a girl?''

''It's a girl!'' came the reply.

Indira walked out slowly to greet the crowds.

Noticing her rosebud, they were joyful and let out cries
of happiness, ''The rosebud returns!''

They, too, remembered her father.

8

2

Blessings on Indira

About the year 1900, Indira's grandparents and father moved to a large house in the rich section of the city of Allahabad. Grandpa Motilal, Grandma Swarup, and their son, Jawahar, who was then ten years old, loved the house at first sight.

The mansion was named ANAND BHAVAN or *House of Joy*. It was a warm, friendly place with people always coming and going enjoying the friendship, food, and fun of the Nehrus. The Nehrus were part of a very small group of Indians allowed to mix with the British who governed India. Even the British sometimes came to visit.

ANAND BHAVAN was an elegant house, the pride of Motilal.

ANAND BHAVAN spread over a large piece of property. It was surrounded by carefully tended beds of roses and vegetables, lemon trees, mango trees, and a neatly kept lawn. The outdoor tennis court, indoor swimming pool, riding stables, and dog kennels were used by family and friends.

Like a ray of sunshine, Jawahar was always warm and friendly. He enjoyed being with people, and they with him. His father wanted him to have the best education possible, so he decided to send his son to England for high school and college. Nothing was too good for his son.

When the handsome Jawahar returned home as a
lawyer, the parents of many girls wanted him to marry
their daughters. The most beautiful girl, Kamala Kaul,
was chosen as his bride-to-be. She was tiny, shy, and very
religious. No expense was spared in making their wedding
a beautiful affair. Three hundred guests travelled by train
to the bride's home town where tents were set up in the
Nehru wedding camp. Celebrations lasted for three days.

The couple returned to ANAND BHAVAN, and before
long they were happily expecting their first child.
November 19, 1917, dawned bright and sunny. On that
day their only daughter, Indira, was born.

Grandma Swarup could not hide her disappointment.

"She should have been a boy!"

Always quick to scold, Grandpa Motilal answered,
"You must not say that! This daughter may be better than
a thousand sons!"

Bundled in a shawl, looking like a china doll with black
ringlets, Indira was carried to the cottage of an old family
servant who was dying of cancer. He took for granted that
the child was a boy and showered it with the prayers and
blessings of a child who was to carry on the family name.

"By God's grace," he prayed, "through this child the
Nehru name will live forever."

3

Love and Duty

When Indira was born, a new mood was taking hold of the Indian people. Having been ruled by outsiders for many years, they wanted to govern themselves. They began to resent their harsh and cruel treatment by the British.

They remembered that Americans had fought a war against the British and had won their independence. So could the Indian people. Their war, however, would be different. It would not be fought with guns but in three other ways:

First, the people would not obey unjust laws.

Second, they would refuse to pay taxes to the British.

Third, they would use only goods made in India.

Curly-locked Indira finds the lap of her mother a cozy place to be on her first birthday.

India's spiritual leader, Mahatma Gandhi, was a close family friend. In 1924 he fasted twenty-one days to protest British rule, became ill, and was visited by six year old Indira.

The peaceful war needed plans and direction, so many important men came to ANAND BHAVAN to meet with Motilal and Jawahar. Little Indira sat in on the meetings with her big dark eyes wide with wonder.

"Don't use any foreign-made goods," she heard. "We refuse to be a market place for the goods made in other countries. Everything in our homes, not made in India, must be destroyed."

Indira knew their home was filled with furniture, draperies, and clothing her grandfather had bought on his shopping sprees in Europe. She ran into the hall, called the servants together, jumped on a table, and made a speech of her own, telling them what she heard.

With a sense of duty, the family and servants gathered together the foreign-made goods. Rich velvet draperies and clothing made a beautiful rainbow pile. At night, gathered on the rooftop, they set a fire and watched the blaze until nothing remained but the ashes.

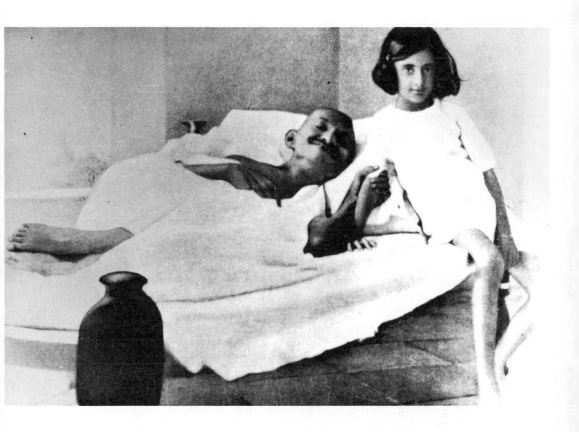

That fire was easy to set, but a few days later Indira had a more difficult decision to make. Her mother called her into the living room to see an aunt who had just returned from France.

"Auntie brought you a dress," she said. "If you like, you may wear it."

The new embroidered dress was lovely, and Indira put out her hand to receive it. Suddenly she stopped.

"No, thank you," she said quietly. "I can't accept it."

"Why not?" her aunt wanted to know.

"Because I want to help India. I must not use anything made in another country," she answered.

"Then why, my dear child, are you playing with that foreign doll?"

What was she saying? "Foreign doll?" What "foreign doll?" Indira looked at the doll in her arms. It had been made in England, but it was her favorite. It was no "foreign doll" to her.

"This is my friend, and I LOVE HER!" she shouted as she ran from the room.

At that moment she felt a terrible battle raging inside, a fight between love for the doll and duty toward her country. She loved her doll, but she knew she had to help India. That evening she did not eat supper, and in bed she tossed and turned. Finally she knew what she had to do.

She crawled out of bed, took the doll, and went outdoors. There, crying her heart out, she set fire to her "foreign doll." Then she turned and ran away quickly.

To this day, Indira hates striking a match.

18

4

Peaceful War

When Indira was four years old, the British put the Nehru men and their followers in jail for the first time. Jailing them was the only way to stop their activities. Although the men did not mind, Indira could never accept the loneliness she felt as she wandered around her home. Without the hearty laughs and bear hugs of the two big men in her life, she sometimes thought her heart would break.

Many times in years to follow she was to be awakened by soldiers coming to lead off members of her family. Accepting arrests peacefully was another way to resist the British.

ANAND BHAVAN was the home of the large family pictured here. Standing are Indira's father, two aunts, Indira, and her uncle. Seated are Indira's grandmother, grandfather, and mother.

While in prison, her father, too, was lonely. As he wrote many long letters, sharing his thoughts and love, he felt closer to his family.

"You are very fortunate in having a brave and wonderful mummie," he once wrote to Indira, "and if you are ever in doubt or in trouble, you cannot have a better friend."

Indira's mother was indeed wonderful. As a child she had been active, happy, and healthy. But tuberculosis left her frail and weak. To be cured, her doctors said, she needed the sunshine and fresh air of Switzerland.

Indira, sitting on the table, was always close
to her father. He holds one of her cousins on his lap.

After Indira's father was released from prison, the
Nehrus made their first trip to Europe as a family. Indira
was then eight years old. In Europe Kamala rested while
Jawahar and Indira spent time ice skating, skiing, and
having fun in the snow.

With Kamala's health improved, the family returned to
India, and Jawahar again jumped into politics. He was
more sure than ever that India had to throw off the yoke of
Great Britain if it was to have a free and happy future.

Leading marches and demonstrations against the
British, he was sometimes beaten by police with billy
clubs. Bones were broken during the demonstrations, but
the spirit of India was not.

One evening, when Indira was twelve, she sat in the
well stocked library reading the story of Joan of Arc. Joan
had led the French armies against their enemies. Her
story always excited Indira. Putting down the book, Indira
wandered down the long hall to her father's study.

He was busy writing something. Indira settled herself
in a big chair and sat quietly, watching him work. When at
last he finished, he asked her to read what he had written.

*We believe that it is the right of the Indian People, as
of any other people, to have freedom to enjoy the
fruits of their toil and the necessities of life, so that
they may have full opportunities for growth...We
believe therefore that India must break the ties with
Britain and attain complete independence.*

22

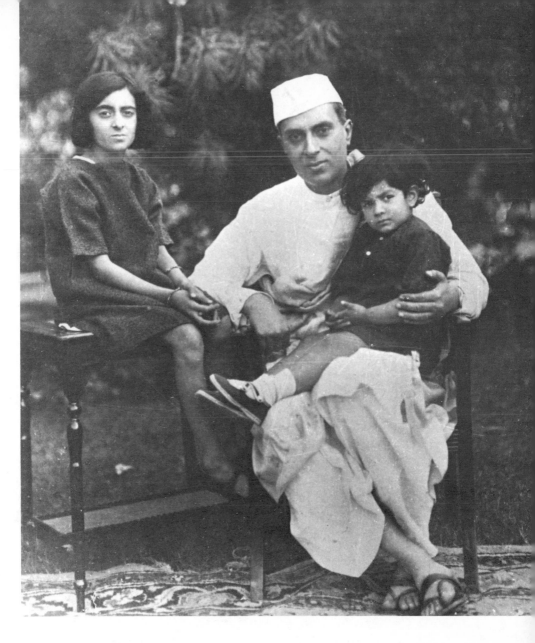

"You read well, Indira. You have just read our new Declaration of Independence. Did you know you are now pledged to India?" her father asked.

"Yes, Papa, and I am proud to be," she answered excitedly.

On January 26, 1930, millions of Indians made their Declaration of Independence and promised to help India win the war against Britain. Jawahar became the nation's great hero and leader.

Chapter 5

A Life of Partings

As time went on, more and more people were arrested for not paying their taxes and for disobeying laws. Indira saw her father, her mother, her grandfather, and her two aunts arrested one by one. Her grandmother was the only person left at ANAND BHAVAN to keep an eye on Indira.

Indira, then thirteen, wanted to be arrested, too, but she was too young. After much thought she decided to form the Monkey Brigade.

They were no monkeys, the six thousand children of Allahabad who formed her group. They were spies and fighters. Jumping rope and playing near police stations, they overheard plans for arrests and raids. Quickly their feet carried them to their adult leaders where the treasured secrets were passed on. Were the police puzzled? You bet. They could not figure out how their plans leaked out. The monkeys knew.

The monkeys helped in the offices, made flags, cooked meals, and gave first aid. They freed the grownups for other work.

The name of the group came from a story once told to Indira. It seems that monkeys helped Rama, the hero, reach his wife who had been taken to the neighboring island of Ceylon. The monkeys formed a bridge so Rama could cross over from India and rescue her. Like those monkeys, Indira and her friends felt they were bridges between the Indian leaders.

Grandpa Motilal had been a very rich and successful lawyer. He had a quick temper and was usually headstrong and bossy. But with Indira he was tender and loving. Even Indira's parents worried about how he was spoiling her.

As a young girl, Indira was often timid and lonely.

His death, when Indira was fourteen, deeply saddened her. To make matters worse, her father was again sent to prison, and her mother moved to a far away city for medical treatment. Indira had a hollow feeling in her stomach when she left for Poona to attend a new high school.

At Poona she cried buckets of tears, standing behind a tree where no one could see or hear her. Would her family ever be together again, she wondered. When three cousins joined her at Poona after their mother was arrested, Indira felt less alone.

Her loneliness always vanished for a moment when she was running hard and fast. Nothing so thrilled her. She could beat almost anyone in school races. Mountain climbing, though, was her favorite sport. She jumped at the chance for a field trip or a picnic in the mountains.

By the time she finished high school, her family's
money was almost gone. Police had raided ANAND
BHAVAN and taken most of the movable property to
make up for the taxes Jawahar refused to pay. The only
valuables which her parents still owned were her
mother's jewels. Finally the precious stones had to be sold
for her mother's medical treatment and her own college
education.

After graduation her teary-eyed classmates saw her off
at a train station. She headed for Calcutta to live with her
mother in an apartment. Her father was in a nearby jail.
She and her mother were often taken for sisters.

Every two weeks they could visit her father for twenty
minutes. It was such a short time in which to say so much.
But it was better than nothing.

A new school year began. Indira enrolled at a quiet place run by India's greatest poet, Tagore. He had won a Nobel prize for his writing. Classes were held under the trees, and students learned from the many faces of nature. At that school she found a peace and happiness she had never known before. She also learned a new love for poetry and music. Before the year ended, she was again called home to accompany her sick mother to Europe.

Neither the best doctors nor the clean air of the Black Forest in Germany could cure Kamala. She was transferred to a hospital in Switzerland. There was no improvement. Jawahar was released from prison to be with his wife and daughter. On February 28, 1936, the lovely, quiet woman of courage died, leaving two sad people to mourn her and to comfort each other.

To England and Home Again

After a few days together, Jawahar left for India and his work while Indira went to England to begin her school there. Being short of money, she shared an apartment with a schoolmate from Poona named Shanta Gandhi. They enjoyed being on their own in a new country.

Through scrimping and saving, they managed to attend a few concerts and plays. Once in awhile they even ate at a restaurant. One day Indira introduced Shanta to a childhood friend, Feroze Gandhi, who came from her home city. He was dark and very good looking. Shanta thought she saw a special friendship growing between Indira and her friend.

**She blossomed into young womanhood
in Switzerland where this photo was taken.**

The Second World War was raging, and every student
in London seemed to be active in some political
movement. Indira joined the Indian League which was
trying to convince English people that India needed its
independence.

Indira, like her mother, was somewhat thin and frail.
One day, while out hiking, she was caught in a heavy
downpour of rain. She came home soaked and caught a
dreadful chest cold. When the cold turned to pleurisy, she
was sent to Switzerland to recover. She stayed there
almost a year to get well and to avoid the bombs being
dropped on London by the Germans.

After a year she knew she wanted to return to India —
and soon. Her friend, Feroze, promised to travel with her.
The seas were full of warships and submarines, so the trip
was filled with risks and dangers. But Indira knew she had
to go home.

33

**Indira became more and more sure of
herself, happy that she was a woman.**

Their ship docked at a city in South Africa called
Durban. It was to remain there a week. Indira was greeted
with cheers of welcome from the members of the Indian
community there. She was known as their beloved
Nehru's daughter. The community had planned a
reception for her, but she wanted no part of it. She was
asked to give a speech, but she shied away from doing
that.

She and Feroze were taken on a tour of the city the next
day. What she saw horrified her. The black people were
separated from others by a policy of apartheid. Their
living conditions were worse than anything she had ever
seen. Indira's anger rose to new heights. When she was
again invited to the reception and asked to give a speech,
she accepted.

The Indians expected a few sweet words, but they received a severe tongue lashing. She harshly criticized the treatment of the blacks. She said it was like the cruel treatment of the Jews in Germany.

She lost friends during that speech. Her warm welcome turned icy cold, and she was ignored the remainder of the week her ship was in port.

Indira learned one important lesson that day. She could give a speech when she had something she really wanted to say.

7 Chapter

Wedding Bells

Feroze had been like a son to Indira's mother. He was always welcome at ANAND BHAVAN and had grown active in the freedom movement. Jawahar was his idol. During the many days of Kamala's illness, Feroze often cared for her. When she was hospitalized in Europe, he managed to leave his studies to spend time with her. When he was still in his teens, he asked Kamala if she would give him permission to marry Indira.

Kamala had answered, ''Yes, if she comes to love you.''

Feroze and Indira had come to know and love each
other in England. They decided to marry when they
returned to India. When they arrived home, Jawahar was
in prison again, so they kept their romance a secret for
months. People seeing them together thought they were
just good friends, but Indira and Feroze knew they were in
love.

One day a paper leaked the news of their upcoming
wedding. The whole country seemed to rise up in arms.
People were worried because Indira, a Hindu of the
highest caste, was planning to marry a man from Persia, a
Parsi, who followed the religion of Zoroaster.

Letters of angers and threats came to ANAND
BHAVAN. No one wanted the marriage. Feroze had little
money, and people said the marriage could not possibly
work. Even Indira's father had problems accepting the
marriage.

Once Indira had made up her mind, there was no
changing it! She pointed out to her father that he was
always preaching a new India based on equality, no
matter what the caste or religion.

Jawahar knew that no society could survive if money,
class, or religion were a test of a person's worth. He
finally accepted and helped his people accept the fact of
the marriage.

After years of neglect, ANAND BHAVAN once again
became a busy nest of activity. Preparations were made
for the wedding. Gifts and letters poured in from the
whole country. Indira happily attended to details.

March 26, 1942, finally arrived. Indira's wedding dress
was a pink sari made of yarn spun by her father in prison.
Her bracelets, necklaces, and earrings were of leaves and
flowers. Her father, just out of prison, gave her away by
placing her hand in the hand of the groom. Prayers were
said, and a fire was lit into which the priests poured butter
with a silver spoon. Feroze and Indira walked around the
fire seven times to seal their union. Finally flower petals
were showered on them as joyful songs were sung.

They left for Kashmir on their honeymoon. Together they made plans for the future. Little did they know that within a few short months they would be separated by imprisonment.

8

Freedom at Last

Jawahar was imprisoned for the last time in August of 1942. Feroze was also in and out of jail, hiding in disguise and carrying on his work. When soldiers came to ANAND BHAVAN and arrested her aunt in the middle of the night, Indira knew that her arrest would soon follow. When she was asked to speak at a public meeting, she went prepared to go directly to prison. Truckloads of soldiers came as soon as she began to speak. She and several others were loaded into trucks and taken to jail.

Her aunt and cousin welcomed her to the prison. With no flowers, sky, or grass in sight, the prison was colorless and drab. Indira was sick for most of the nine months she was in prison. When she was finally released, she went right home to bed in the deserted ANAND BHAVAN. A few months later her husband, who had been imprisoned, was also released. Finally they had some peaceful months together. Their first son, Rajiv, was born in August of 1944.

Radiant Indira enjoys her two little boys, Rajiv and Sanjay.

Her father was released in June of 1945 after spending a total of almost nine years behind jail walls. In 1945 Great Britain made the decision for which everyone had been waiting: they would turn the government over to its own people. The peaceful war had been won. Jawahar was named India's first prime minister and told to form a new government.

Plans were made to divide India into two countries, Pakistan for the Moslems and India for the Hindus. Because some Hindus lived in Pakistan and some Moslems lived in India, religious anger caused riots to flare up all over the country.

The second son of Indira and Feroze was born in December of 1946. He was given the name Sanjay. Before Indira was completely strong again, she was out among the people trying to quiet their anger and still their hatreds. If she or her father turned up at the scene of a riot, the mood suddenly seemed to change. The people listened to the Nehrus.

After two years of planning, work, and struggle, the Indian people were ready to assume the responsibility of self government on August 15, 1947.

When the eve of that great day arrived, Prime Minister Nehru addressed the nation.

*At the stroke of midnight, when the world sleeps,
India will wake to life and freedom.*

The Indians, full of pride, knew their struggles had earned them the right to govern themselves.

9

Joy and Sadness

The Prime Minister moved to a large house, once owned by the British, in the capital city of New Delhi. He knew his new home could never be as warm as ANAND BHAVAN. He missed his wife Kamala. Would they someday meet again?

He asked Indira to be his hostess and companion. Her work was cut out for her. The first thing she did was remove the large pictures of British officers which lined the walls. Then she used her own decorator's touch to beautify the home.

In 1956 President and Mrs. Eisenhower welcomed Prime Minister Nehru and his daughter, Indira Gandhi.

She tended the countless guests who came from all over the world. She watched over the meal preparation, being careful that all religious beliefs were respected and that guests were served what they could eat. That was no easy matter. Some guests were Hindu and would eat no beef. Moslems would eat no pork. Others would eat no meat at all. Some had to be served before noon; others could not eat until after 1:30 p.m. Somehow Indira managed to keep the home running smoothly.

The Prime Minister, wearing a rose, and Indira were met by President John F. Kennedy.

She travelled to almost every large country with her father. He met with leaders, and she listened and learned. What a preparation for the day when she would take his place as prime minister.

Indira often had to remind her father to eat, and sometimes she insisted that he get to bed. As leader of the new nation, he often felt helpless in wiping out the religious hatreds of his people. He needed Indira as his friend and support. She learned to be a good listener.

Her father loved Rajiv and Sanjay and enjoyed his most restful moments playing with them at lunch time or before bed. He shared his home with three tiger cubs until they were so big they had to be sent to a zoo. Rajiv and Sanjay never tired of watching their grandpa stand on his head each morning. He did that almost to the day he died.

Politics also drew Feroze into the arena, and he gave it everything he had. No wonder he suffered a heart attack in 1959. The doctors warned him to take it easy, but he could not. One day in 1960 while he was home alone and Indira was out of town, he had his second attack. Although the doctor insisted that he stay in bed, he drove himself to the hospital. There, while pouring himself a cup of tea, he collapsed. A few hours later he died, his promising future cut short. Indira was a widow at age forty-three.

The burden of the country weighed heavily on her father's shoulders. India's war with China in 1962 seemed to age him ten years overnight. In January, 1964, at the age of seventy-four, he collapsed. By May he was feeling better. He took a weekend trip by helicopter to a nearby town. The following Monday, he awoke, shaved, and complained of a pain. While talking to Indira, he fell into a coma. Six hours later he died as a result of a stroke. News of his death spread quickly to his people.

"Our light has gone out!" they cried. "We are like lost sheep; the captain of our ship is gone."

Hundreds of thousands left their villages to walk miles to his funeral. Although divided by religions, cultures, and language, the people were united in the loss of their father and leader. His death left a great emptiness in their lives.

His body was covered with 700 roses and placed on a carriage to be pulled by 60 soldiers and sailors. Millions lined the route of the funeral procession.

50

At the edge of the Jumna River, his body was cremated. His people prayed, sang, and mourned. Twenty-four hours later his ashes were gathered and spread over the sacred Ganges River where the ashes of his parents and wife were also spread.

10

A Most Powerful Woman

A man named Shastri succeeded Jawaharlal Nehru. In two years time he, too, was dead, the victim of a heart attack.

In January of 1966, Indira was elected Prime Minister. She had been chosen as the Congress Party's candidate. Some politicans thought she could be pushed around easily since she was shy and appeared indecisive at times. In 1969, some party leaders made plans to replace her with another candidate. She seemed to play right into their hands even as they tried to remove her. One day she suddenly threw her support to a candidate of her own. She backed such a campaign supporting him for office that her man won in a landslide, and the old party leaders were left dizzy. Indira capped that victory by her own reelection as Prime Minister in 1971. She received two-thirds of the votes, an unheard-of majority.

Two handsome sons, Rajiv (center) and Sanjay, are on hand to welcome their mother when she returns from her travels. Rajiv is a pilot for Indian Airlines while Sanjay designs low-cost automobiles.

The Prime Minister dedicates a new home for the homeless children of the capital city, New Delhi.

As Prime Minister, she is a busy lady. She rises at six, reads the newspapers, and eats breakfast. At eight o'clock she looks over the business of the day while visitors gather on the lawn. As she meets people, she gives the traditional greeting with a smile. She joyfully receives their gifts of flowers which she loves. Problems and complaints, ranging from straying sacred cows to police brutality, are listened to thoughtfully. By eleven o'clock she is in her office receiving more callers, attending meetings, and facing difficult decisions.

She leads a country of 600,000,000 people, one-seventh of the world's total population. In 1971 220,000,000 Indians lived below the poverty level of twenty cents a day. By 1975 the number had grown to 385,000,000. Unemployment is a staggering problem with 30,000,000 out of work. One out of three college graduates cannot find jobs, and six times more farm workers are out of work than ten years ago.

The problems which plague the nation are simply
enormous. Three continuous years of dry weather have
caused grain shortages and starvation. Factories run at
less than full capacity, and black market operations push
prices sky high. Corruption, cheating, failure of
leadership, and violent outbreaks create chaos. In the
midst of it all, eyes look to Indira Gandhi for leadership.
Her appearance deceives. She looks frail, lovely, and
gentle, but she is strong, powerful, and determined. She
seldom argues with anyone. Instead she sits silently
absorbing what she hears. Few know what she is thinking.

She loves her people with a passion and wants them to
be as strong as they were when they faced billy clubs in
their fight for freedom from the British.

During the five months when she is not meeting with
Parliament, she travels to remote parts of India. There she
speaks to the people with the hot sun blazing over the
jungles and the fields of tea.

She reminds her people that their freedom has been
bought at a great price.

"It is your duty and privilege to serve it well," she
says.

11

Crisis of 1975

The summer of 1975 brought Prime Minister Gandhi to the most difficult stage of her political career. On June 12, a judge in her home state of Allahabad ruled she had violated the country's election laws when she campaigned for office.

Calls for nationwide civil disobedience were immediately sent out by her opponents who wanted her removed from office. Mrs. Gandhi acted with swift determination. She declared a state of national emergency and ordered the arrest of her political enemies. Then she imposed strict censorship on the press. She defended her actions by saying that the state of emergency was necessary for the safety of the country and that it was provided for in the Indian Constitution.

While campaigning in 1971, Indira joins folk dancers in making music.

After presenting the important lady a
bouquet of flowers, a little girl is comforted
by Mrs. Gandhi. She cannot seem
to spot her mother in the crowd.

The whole world responded with outrage, especially
because of the press censorship. No criticism of the
conditions in India were allowed in the country. She was
accused of turning her back on democracy, and headlines
screamed, *Freedom Lost in Democratic India*.

"The opposition has only one aim, to destroy me," she
insisted. "They have no other program to help the
country. I must do my duty to safeguard the nation."

The country split into two camps. Some called for her
forced resignation. Others supported her, calling her the
Goddess of India. They gathered outside her home
singing, "We will face bullets, but we will support you."

The big question was whether Mrs. Gandhi took the
drastic measures in order to pave the way for needed
reforms in her country, or whether she was merely
protecting her own power against her critics.

60

Arresting her opponents seemed to be in direct contradiction to democracy, government by the people.

"While it is the responsibility of the government not to suppress the opposition, it is also the responsibility of the opposition not to interfere with the running of the government," she said.

As the summer passed and the dust settled, the sensational headlines disappeared. Editorialists and speakers began to come to her support. Some admitted that democracy as known in the United States was probably different than in India where 50% of the population could not read or write and 80% were living in poverty. The country was in such a state of disorder and chaos that democracy, as known in the West, seemed somewhat out of the question.

A Nobel Peace prize winner was quoted as saying, "Rights of individuals are luxuries that India can perhaps ill afford."

As fall led into winter, the big question continued to be, "Democracy or dictatorship for India?"

The words of Indira are clear. "Would I want to be known in history as the person who defeated the most cherished hopes of my father, Jawaharlal Nehru, for the Indian people?"

Only time will tell. History will decide.

62

CAROL BAUER CHURCH is a graduate of the College of
St. Catherine in St. Paul, Minnesota. She is a former
school teacher and lives with her husband Jim and
daughter Laura. She is currently working on additional
titles for the **Focus on Famous Women Series**.